my guide to space exploration

Astronaut

Cherry Lake Press

Published in the United States of America by Cherry Lake Publishing Group
Ann Arbor, Michigan
www.cherrylakepublishing.com

Reading Adviser: Beth Walker Gambro, MS, Ed., Reading Consultant, Yorkville, IL
Book Design: Jennifer Wahi
Illustrator: Joseph Hatch

Photo Credits: © Andrei Armiagov/Shutterstock, 5; NASA/James Blair, 7; NASA, 9; NASA/Reid Wiseman, 11; © Aiartcreations2020/Dreamstime.com, 13; NASA/Otis Imboden, 15; © Science History Images/Alamy Stock Photo, 17; NASA, 19; NASA/Kjell Lindgren, 21; NASA, 23

Cherry Lake Press is an imprint of Cherry Lake Publishing Group

Library of Congress Cataloging-in-Publication Data has been filed and is available at catalog.loc.gov

Printed in the United States of America

table of contents

About the author: Samantha Bell was born and raised near Orlando, Florida. She grew up in a family of eight kids and all kinds of pets, including goats, chickens, cats, dogs, rabbits, horses, parakeets, hamsters, guinea pigs, a monkey, a raccoon, and a coatimundi. She now lives with her family in the foothills of the Blue Ridge Mountains, where she enjoys hiking, painting, and snuggling with their cats Pocket, Pebble, and Mr. Tree-Tree Triggers.

About the illustrator: Joseph Hatch is the art director for Tilbury House Publishers. He holds a degree in Graphic Design and Illustration from Madison College in Madison, Wisconsin. An illustrator, painter, and certified Michigan master naturalist, Joseph can usually be found at home organic gardening, beekeeping, growing edible mushrooms, planting native plants, and either building, fixing, or playing stringed instruments. He lives in Ann Arbor, Michigan, with his wife, their two children, a house cat, two dogs, nine chickens, and fifty thousand honeybees.

About Astronauts

I'm an astronaut. I explore space.

I train. I can live and work in space.

I do many jobs. I fix things inside the **spacecraft**. I go on **space walks**. I make repairs outside.

I do **experiments**. I learn more about space.

JAXA

I wear special clothes. It is called a space suit.

My spacecraft moves fast. It goes around Earth. There is no **gravity**. Everything inside floats. I float, too.

My food floats in cans and packages. I attach it to the table to eat.

Punch
PTAP
Green Tea
w/Sugar

I exercise every day. It keeps my **muscles** strong.

I use a **radio**. I talk to the team on Earth. I also talk to family and friends. I can use email and make video calls, too.

I’m ready for my next **mission**!

CAUTION
TURN OFF STROBE LIGHT WHEN TAXIING NEAR OTHER AIRCRAFT OR WHEN FLYING IN FOG OR CLOUDS. STANDARD POSITION LIGHTS MUST BE USED FOR ALL NIGHT OPERATIONS
ALTERNATOR
LANDING LT.
TAXI
NAV
EXTENDED
RETRACT
OPEN

glossary & index

glossary

experiments (ex-PAIR-uh-mentz) carefully planned tests to discover something unknown

gravity (GRAA-vuh-tee) an invisible force that pulls objects toward each other

mission (MIH-shuhn) an important job that a person is sent out to do

muscles (MUH-suhlz) the parts of the body that make it possible for people to move

radio (RAY-dee-oh) a device that sends and receives direct electronic signals

spacecraft (SPAYS-kraft) a vehicle made to travel in outer space

space walks (SPAYS WAWKS) moving around outside a spacecraft in outer space

index